HOW TO BE A
Writer
WITHOUT WRITING
a Book

LORRIE NICOLES
Tora Writing Services

APOCRYPHILE
PRESS

Apocryphile Press
1700 Shattuck Ave #81
Berkeley, CA 94709
www.apocryphilepress.com

Copyright © 2020 Lorrie Nicoles, Tora Writing Services.
All Rights Reserved
Printed in the United States of America

ISBN 978-1-949643-33-6 | paperback
ISBN 978-1-949643-34-3 | epub

All rights reserved. No part of this book may be reproduced, stored in a retrieval system, or transmitted in any form or by any means—electronic, mechanical, photocopy, recording, or otherwise—without written permission of the author and publisher, except for brief quotations in printed reviews.

NOTICE: Tora Writing Services cannot guarantee the functionality of any links in this book.

Please join our mailing list at
www.apocryphilepress.com/free
We'll keep you up-to-date on all our new releases,
and we'll also send you a FREE BOOK. Visit us today!

Contents

Oh, the Irony!..1
   What You'll Find...3
What Qualifies Me to Write a Book?..5
   The Early Years...5
   The Engineering Years..7
   Tech Writing, No Books Involved 8
   From Tech Writer to Writer 9
      Writer v. Author 10
   Contributors.. 10
   Disclaimer.. 11
What, You Don't Write Just Anything?... 13
   Grant Writers 14
   Writing for Businesses 16
      Marketing/Advertising Writers 16
      Technical Writers 23
      Electronic Communications...25
   Writing to Explain 26
      Explanatory Writers..26
      Medical Writers...28
      Science Writers... 30
   Writing for Individuals 31
      Resume Writers... 31
      Speech Writers 33
   Travel Writers 36

- To Edit, or Not to Edit – Is Not the Question 39
  - What You Say v What You Mean 40
  - But That's So Obvious 40
  - Why an Editor? 41
- What Do You Mean, "Type of Editor"? 43
  - Developmental Editing 45
  - Copy Editing 46
  - Line Editing 47
  - So, What Kind of Editing Do I Do? 48
- So You Want to Write and/or Edit 49
  - In General 49
    - Appreciate Your Value 49
    - Don't Take Yourself Too Seriously 50
    - Impress People with Your Ability, Not Your Vocabulary ... 50
    - Learn from Criticism 51
    - If You Love to Write, Then Write 52
  - As an Independent 52
    - Define Your 3 Ps of Business 52
    - Appreciate Your Value – II 55
    - Feel Free to Mix and Match 56
    - Protect Yourself 57
    - The Client Is the Boss – Until You Fire 'Em 61
    - Continue to Build Yourself 62
    - Don't (Always) Work at Home 63
    - The Rest: Don't Ask; I'm Still Working on It. 64
- The Continuation of the Path 67
  - Living on the Corner of What I Love and What I'm Good At ... 67
- Contributors 69
  - Additional Readers 73

Oh, the Irony!

I'm one of those people who can't define "irony" but knows when it hits me over the head with a brick. Although I am likely to miss the more subtle examples, even I see the irony in a book with the title *How to Be a Writer without Writing a Book*.

Let's back up: I am a writer who never planned to write a book. (Actually, I'm a writer and editor – the distinction will become clear later.) So how is it that you are reading a book by me? Personal development and sarcasm is how.

As part of my business and personal development, I participate in multiple mastermind groups. In one group, I asked for suggestions on how I could generate passive income (that stuff that makes you money without ongoing work). Workshops, webinars, and such came up. Then one member brought up the fact that he considered my work – web copy, blogs, newsletters, articles, and editing – very niche and maybe I could make something out of that. In a fit of perfectly timed sarcasm, I said, "What, write a book called *How to Be a Writer without Writing a Book*?" My title was born.

While I REALLY did not want to write a book, that damn title haunted me. Additionally, I had no clue as to what I would fill a book with. OK, that's not entirely true, but my picture book called *Toilets around the World: How Do I Flush This Thing?* is not what I'm talking about here.

Knowing I needed help, I reached out to my friend, Sue Stoney, *The Message Crafter*. Sue is a collaborative coach helping people write their books. Of course, she didn't tell me what to put in the book. Instead, she asked me two questions:

- Who's your audience?
- What's the purpose of the book? Specifically, why this topic now?

Once I got past the deer-in-the-headlights feeling, I could positively answer:

I DON'T KNOW!!!!!

I did know that I love the big old brick of irony that is the title.

I also knew that writing a book would not actually make me money; however, it would increase my credibility, and that would be profitable.

Personal and business development has done something else for me. It has taught me to be aware of when my own "little voice" is getting in my way. At those times, I'm much better at saying, "Thank you for sharing; now shut up."

After talking to a couple of other friends/coaches (Sydney Metrick of *Artful Coaching* and Elaine Betts of *Go Far Consulting*) I came up with some ideas and uncomplicated my approach. (Turns out that "because the title won't leave me alone" is a reasonable answer to "why this topic now.")

And suddenly, I was no longer at I DON'T KNOW!!!!!

I'd moved to I'm Not Totally Sure, But I've Got an Idea.

The true moral of the story is: Life is a team effort – have friends, have coaches, and have some of them be both.

What You'll Find

Big picture, I want people to understand that it is possible to earn a living by writing – without writing a book. Specifically:

1. What are some of the different types of writing that pay people?
2. What are the different types of editing?
3. What's the difference between working on staff at a company and working for yourself?
   a. And if you're going to do this working for yourself, how does that work?

Before you ask, I do not directly address how to gain staff positions. Here's my advice: know your skills, know how to interview, and know people who can introduce you to people who are hiring. That last one can take time, and I know a guy who can help you out if you'd like a referral.

> **Food for Thought**
>
> "Only kings, presidents, editors, and people with tapeworms have the right to use the editorial 'we'."
> — Mark Twain

What Qualifies Me to Write a Book?

Even though I had the determination and the content, that voice in my head kept telling me that I wasn't actually qualified. To which I've decided to respond,

> *Food for Thought*
>
> "If a word in the dictionary were misspelled, how would we know?"
> — Steve Wright

"Who is?" You don't know until you do it or don't do it.

Part of what makes me good at what I do is the path I travelled to get here. I believe that understanding some of a person's history gives context to the advice that person gives. I want you to have context for this book.

Few of us end up being what we envisioned as kids. I'm not sure if I ever saw myself as a writer. Regardless, I've taken some amusing detours in life – but that's a good thing. They add to my skill set.

I bet your detours make you better at what you do too.

The Early Years

We are a collection of experiences. The ones that happen early in life – when we have little control and less understanding – tend to make the most impact. For me, my parents' divorce –

specifically the ongoing ramifications – was the biggest event of my "formative" years. Some of those ramifications included: a tendency to make decisions that I thought would please, or one up, my dad; a great deal of independence; and a step-mom I consider my third parent – all of whom are amazing in different ways.

I'm proud of the excellent education I got from the Oakland Public School System. The adults in my life were well educated, well spoken, and primed for debate – and my teachers continued the trend. So did some of my amazingly whip-smart classmates. All of that combined meant that I wrote, and wrote, and wrote. Being on the high-school paper for two years allowed me to write (and edit) some more. I also realized my passion for Clear Communication (yes, that is supposed to be capitalized). It amazed me how few of those whip-smart kids could explain themselves, in speech or in writing. They might have been smarter than me, but I could make my point – people understood me when I explained something.

Stir into the mix:
- considerable exposure to different thoughts and viewpoints;
- my sister as my best friend;
- volunteering in my mom's chosen self-help group into high school; and
- becoming a certified white-water raft guide and backpack leader for the Sierra Club's inner-city outreach program.

It is safe to say that I started college having had many experiences, some of it even practical.

The Engineering Years

One of those Dad decisions was that I would get an Engineering degree from UC Berkeley.

Many people are surprised that I have an engineering degree. The truth is that getting that degree and the short time I spent in the field set my passion for Clear Communication on fire and is the foundation for many of the successes in my life.

My determination to get an Engineering degree from Berkeley landed me in the mining program. I loved it, and it certainly added to my collection of interesting experiences. The first thing I learned is that graduate students generally make better undergraduate teachers than professors with PhDs – by the time people reach that level of expertise, they tend to have a hard time simplifying their topic enough.

With my Engineering degree in hand, I moved to South Dakota to work for the Homestake Gold Mine. In mining circles, Homestake was a BIG deal. The company was known for chewing up engineers, but if I could last for five years, I could write my ticket to anything I wanted. I lasted two. However, I did end up with a contract at the company's California property, so they paid for the return trip.

I now had six months to figure things out. What I figured out was that I didn't want to live in the back of beyond, and continuing my mining career would mean that I would have to do just that. If I wasn't going to stick with mining, I needed to find something else – quick.

Here's what I knew – because I'd done it repeatedly – I could learn software with limited instruction, then turn around and teach it to other people.

In the job world, who you know will open more doors than what you know. What you know comes into play later. Lucky for me, I knew a very big name in the petrochemical plant software world. He gave me a list of names, and I managed to convince a small company in the Silicon Valley that I could become their user expert.

Suddenly, I was back on the writing path.

Tech Writing, No Books Involved

My first job as a technical writer was to communicate the software to our clients through documentation, training, support, trade shows, and whatever else that came up. My priority was the client's perspective. In a company of engineers, I was the only one with that priority.

Eventually, I had rewritten the manual – but no one counts that as a book. I wrote a manual I wished people would write for me: clear, instructions where I needed instructions, lots of figures, explanations for everything, and no useless fluff. My clients complimented me frequently on my ability to explain the software to them without making them feel stupid. The biggest compliment I got was from a Korean client who told me that he was able to learn the software from the manual, that my manual was very good. Keep in mind, that manual was in English – it was never translated.

I spent close to 15 years as a tech writer; no one asked me if I wrote books.

From Tech Writer to Writer

In 2009, I found myself unemployed. While my engineering detour was an asset when I worked for engineering companies, it made things complicated for my job hunt. In one year, I landed several phone calls and three interviews. Apparently, interviewers had a hard time understanding why I thought I could write about their software when my experience was so specialized. I wondered why they thought I couldn't.

After a technical recruiter forgot I existed for a week, my sister made a joke about me going into the direct sales chocolate business. Instead, I decided to host a chocolate party and was so unimpressed by the consultant that I joined up out of spite. I did home chocolate tasting parties – most of them including chocolate martinis. It was a blast! As fun as it was, it's hard not to notice that being a representative of the chocolate equivalent to Tupperware® is a whopper of a detour from writing.

As part of building my chocolate business, I joined the referral networking group BNI® (Business Networking International). That is where I met Gail Nott, who does online marketing. We were having a "get to know you" chat that included my writing history. Gail mentioned that some of her clients needed help with blog writing; did I think I could do that? In my head, I said, "Blog? What the hell goes in a blog?" What Gail heard was, "Sure!" I ended up writing for several of her clients.

Officially, my primary job was selling chocolate, and the writing was just a side thing. The problem was that I needed to do better financially and was having a hard time figuring out how to make chocolate do that. Then Gail suggested that maybe I shouldn't do as much writing for her. The light bulb turned on with a resounding DING!

That was on a Monday morning. By my Friday BNI meeting, I had the domain, tag line, 3 Commandments of Writing, a request in to the graphic designer for business card ideas, and was ready to do the paper work to change from The Chocolate Lady to writing services. On top of that, I had multiple people come up to me and say, "You look great! What's going on?" Oh, not much, just an emotional revolution.

And ♪Ta Da♪ Tora Writing Services went from something only Gail knew about to a real live business!

(NOTE TO READER: Tora is the Kanji character for tiger. I use that character for my logo. The why of that is more information than you really need.)

Writer v. Author

In the beginning, when people asked what I did, and I would tell them that I'm a writer, the next question was generally, "Oh? What genre?" *If I wrote books, I'd introduce myself as an "author," not a "writer"!* (As much as I want to, I have yet to yell that at someone. I'm sure it would include a "You moron!" and that just wouldn't do.) Now I say I'm a writer/editor for business owners. That tends to bypass the genre discussion.

Contributors

After the path I've taken in life, what next qualifies me to write this book is my willingness to access the expertise of others. I know of other types of writing; that does not mean I know about them.

Because many types of writing can generate income without creating a book, I decided to tap my network for support. With my membership in global business and professional organizations, I have access to writers around the world. Because culture has such a huge influence on writing, I decided to keep my search to the United States, and I found a handful of writers and editors with specialties other than mine willing to help me. Without these contributors, there would be significantly less variety in the number of specialties covered. While this book is not all-inclusive, I'm proud of the collection in "What, You Don't Write Just Anything?".

The end section, "Contributors," contains a full roster of the writers and editors who lent me some of their brains.

Disclaimer

In life, I'm fairly liberal with curse words. Sometimes I try to censor myself, but normally I just let them fly.

In writing, however, I try not to swear. While some people find swearing offensive, or just inappropriate, there is something about the lack of creativity of the basic four-letter word. When in pain, and I need to scream, creativity is not a criterion. Shocked during a conversation also doesn't necessarily call for inventive phrasing. But, if you're taking the time to write, take the time to insult creatively.

So, from this point (this one right here) forward, all instances of "foul language" – censored or not – come directly from contributors and not me. You'll also note that, in those cases, creative is not called for; down and dirty truth is.

What, You Don't Write Just Anything?

I know several lawyers, and the good ones do one type of law: family, criminal, estate, etc. And they will be the first to tell you that you don't want a criminal lawyer to put your will together!

Like lawyers, writers specialize. Now, the lines are not as definitive between writer types as those between lawyer types, but there are lines.

Before I go into specifics, let me define some things. First, this chapter is about types of nonfiction writing as a way of making a living. Fiction writing is an entirely different thing that lands in the realm of "Not Necessarily Making Money as a Writer." I say that because I find that fiction writers are more likely to write because they need to get the story out and making money (if it sells) is a great side benefit. The types of writing I discuss here are actual ways to make money by putting words together in a written format.

Next, let me repeat that I differentiate between writers and authors. For me, and thus for the purposes of this book, authors write books – fiction or nonfiction. While all authors write, not all writers are authors.

Finally, writers fall into one of two buckets: staff or independent. A staff writer is a person who works for someone else, probably has something resembling regular hours, and takes home a regular paycheck. Independent writers find their own projects, negotiate the pay for each project, and work whatever hours they see fit.

Having been both a staff and independent writer, I can tell you that there is something to be said for each bucket. Being a staff writer has the benefit of regular pay and benefits, along with the possibility of suddenly losing that job. Working for yourself means you get to pick your topics, and chase your topics, and hope to God you have a topic that will pay.

Many people rightly equate "independent" and "freelance." However, I'm beginning to be wary of the term "freelance," because "free" equals no cost. As content writer Susan Shalhoub of *Plum Editorial LLC* in Orlando, FL, said, "Freelancing is really a terrible word for being in business for yourself. It sounds like it's an internship or something. It's certainly not free, and I am not a bank. With writing, it feels especially ironic when a payment is late — generally you've busted your butt to get their deadline met, yet you wait for payment after 30 days."

Grant Writers

(NOTE TO READER: I put Grant Writers first for a few reasons: first, this section turned out to be darn hard to get; second, I mention something here that I refer to later; and third, it is the type of writing people ask most about that I don't do.)

People ask me about grant writing with some regularity, and I always get out of it by saying that I've never written a grant request. The truth is I'm the type who would feel responsible if the organization didn't get the money – I just don't need to do that to myself.

Because grant writing does come up, I was ecstatic when I found Sue Toth of *Sue Toth Writing and Editing Services* in Lake Hopatcong, NJ, and she agreed to contribute. (After receiving Sue's contribution, I started tripping over grant writers left and right.) If nothing else, what Sue had to say about it reinforced my instinctual reluctance to do grant writing.

(SIDE NOTE: in California, it is possible to drive for four to eight hours and never leave the state. Drive that long on the east coast, and you cross multiple state lines! You could fit almost 19 New Jerseys in California! Points I remembered/ figured out while trying to find Lake Hopatcong on the map.)

If you cannot follow the rules (and that's how some of us are), grant writing is not for you. Organizations who offer grants have "extremely specific requirements" around applications – some even to the number of characters used! Straying from the requirements could put an application in the reject pile before anyone even reads it.

If you're good with the rules, the next thing a grant writer needs to be is specific. This is an application for free money; the people giving the money want to know EXACTLY how the organization plans to spend it.

Here is where things can turn difficult. Organizations looking for grants are generally out to do something good that appeals to the funder of the grant. Not only does the money need to be accounted for, that accounting needs to be inspirational. How is what the money will buy going to change the world? Or, as Dalya Massachi of *Writing to Make a Difference* in San Leandro, CA, put it, how is the grant money going to affect the "triple bottom line – people, planet, profits"?

Easy. Sure.

In many ways, grant writing is similar to marketing writing in that: you are advancing the brand of the group the grant is for, you focus on the needs of the reader, and you emphasize the "What's in It for Me" of the readers (why they want to give the grant applicant their money). As I see it, the difference between grants and marketing is that one is for forwarding a purpose while the other is for forwarding a product.

Except for the larger non-profits, organizations that need grant money generally do not have a grant writer on staff. And the organizations that are hiring grant writers are fewer and farther between.

For an independent writer, grant writing can be immensely fulfilling because, as Sue put it, "I feel a much closer bond with my clients than I've ever felt with any boss, because I am truly invested in their success."

Writing for Businesses

Admittedly, most nonfiction, non-book publishing writing (including grant and travel writing) is for a business. The types of writing I cover in this section, though, are specific to doing business.

Marketing/Advertising Writers

All purchases are based on emotion. Logic follows as justification for the purchase. If you are among the many who would argue that point, let me give you a personal example: my continued computer purchases.

My business requires two things: my brain and my computer. Luckily, I don't need to buy the brain. I also don't need to purchase the computers I purchase as frequently as I purchase them. I have a preferred brand. Because I want the mobility of a laptop, I add on the full warranty and replace the thing when that warranty expires rather than risk a problem. Let's look at the emotional words there: preferred, want, and risk. I also believe (another emotion) in buying the best computer possible – a hanger-on from my engineering days.

> *Food for Thought*
>
> "Clutter is the disease of American writing. We are a society strangling in unnecessary words, circular constructions, pompous frills and meaningless jargon."
>
> — William Zinsser
> (author of "On Writing Well")

Even if I didn't have emotions about the specific computer, I sure do about the shopping for it. Only the dead and decomposed do not have some sort of emotion around shopping. Hating to shop may influence more purchases than any other emotion out there. And companies cater to that too.

If you still don't believe that all purchases are emotion-based, look at food. Yes, you need food. Yes, you need to shop for food. Do you buy anything you don't like the taste of? (You will not find a mushroom in my grocery cart.) Are you an all-organic type of guy or dolphin-free tuna type of girl? Do you have an opinion about non-locally-grown produce? The actual food you purchase is a decision based on emotion.

And that is where marketing and advertising come into play.

I separate the two because they have different purposes. The point of marketing is to educate you about a product and get you to like it before you're ready to purchase. Advertising is about getting you to buy this specific item now that you are ready to buy. Both disciplines, however, play on emotion.

The ability to write to emotion is a skill. You want it to be subtle – obvious attempts at manipulation will not go over well. Word choices can be critical. For example, I know someone who loves using the word "compel," and it always grates on me. To me, "compel" implies force, and I am not into being forced into things. Personally, I think "inspire" is much friendlier – and I know that's the point my friend is making. At least she doesn't use "coerce"; that would put significantly more people off.

Marketing and advertising are big employers, from Big Name Corporations to Independent Consultants working in their bunny slippers. Marketing and Advertising consultants frequently do much of the writing themselves, so writing marketing or ad copy as an independent may require you to work with multiple consultants or do some consulting yourself. When I do marketing work, I prefer working with a consultant who has helped the client with a marketing plan. That way the consultant can educate the client about what I will, and will not, deliver.

Humor

While my cousins occasionally think I'm hysterical, we've all got similar crazy genes. Outside of my family, my sense of humor has limited appeal.

And yet, everyone loves a good laugh. So, if you can do that through writing, go for it.

On this topic, I had a huge amount of help from Gene Braunstein of *ComedyFaceLift.com LLC* in Norwalk, CT. (Almost 30 Connecticuts would fit into California.) Before creating ComedyFaceLift.com, which – among other things – helps businesses stand out from their competition by using humor in their marketing, Gene was a stand-up comic, then a sitcom writer/producer in Hollywood. He really does know how to make them laugh.

From Gene I learned that being a staff comedy writer seems to involve a lot of coffee drinking. There are also plenty of brainstorming sessions, story development and refinement, and timing. Network and cable television have time slots and commercials to work within and around – the material has to fit. If you're not one to be bound by timing regulations, there are the unique series from the streaming services (Netflix, Amazon, and such). Then again…while nothing says their episodes need to be specific lengths, they seem to be sticking to the 30- or 60-minute ballpark duration.

All in all, nice work if you can get it. Unfortunately, in Los Angeles apparently "you can go to Costco and for $79.99 you can buy a pallet of sitcom writers and four tires." Translation: there's too much of everyone in LA when it comes to the entertainment industry.

Now, writing humorous content as an independent writer is a different kettle of fish. You must always keep your clients in mind. Their humor is more important than yours. And more import than the client's humor is the humor of the client's audience.

Using humor to tell a story works just as well in business as it does in television. Maybe even more so because your audience isn't safely ensconced on a couch with little incentive to change channels – an engaged reader of your marketing copy is harder to find and keep around. There is, however, a very important rule for this type of humor writing: "Humor shall not f**k with the brand."

Have you ever seen a commercial so funny that you were talking about it the next day? Did you remember what the commercial was for? If so, excellent. If, as happens too often, you remember the joke but not the product, someone needs firing. (Commercials are not cheap!)

People remember experiences that evoke strong emotion. Because most of us would rather remember the happy emotions over the sad, humor is a good way to generate that emotion. However, the point of marketing and advertising is to focus the audience on the product/service. Once you have their attention, you want to convince the audience that their lives will be Oh So Much Better because of the product/service. If the audience only remembers the joke, you have not done your job.

Something about humor that many people may not understand: honesty is required. Randy Wight of *Funny Bone Productions* in Walnut Creek, CA, reminded me of this. Aside from being a marketing genius, as part of his business, Randy teaches people how to use humor in their business. He is also part of an improv group. In all of that, there are three rules he follows:

1. Speak to your audience, not over them.
2. Be vulnerable and honest.
3. Authenticity above everything.

If you think about it, the joke always falls flat when you do not follow those rules.

Story

For a book about non-fiction writing, "Story Writers" might seem a bit of a contradiction. Not true; storytelling is a powerful marketing tool that takes a special type of writer.

The stories I'm talking about are the ones that demonstrate the value – or lack of value – of a product or service by example.

Clyde McDade of *Beach House Creative* in Graham, WA specializes in story email messages that inspire people to buy without pressuring them to buy. Although Clyde limits the types of organizations he helps, his insight – summed up below – is applicable to all story writers.

Rule #1: Tell Powerful Stories. The story of someone's life-altering experience is much more inspiring than a story about day-to-day existence. Good stories can remove sales resistance before someone even feels it.

Think of it this way: Have you ever walked into a store and said, "I want that," purchased it, and left? No comparison shopping, no thought about price, simply "I must have that"? I'm not talking about something prescribed by a doctor or needed for a class. Why did you have to have that item? I'm betting that a story, or a collection of stories, about the majesty of the product did more to convince you than anything else.

> Rule #1-1: Tell Powerful Stories Powerfully. I'll say it again: humans purchase based on emotion and justify

purchases with logic, so appeal to the emotion. One way to evoke emotion is to appeal to all the senses. The bakery didn't just smell good and the cakes look pretty. The scent of freshly melted chocolate floated through the air, and there was a cake decoration for every personality, from regal to whimsical.

Rule #2: Do Not Sell. Tell the story with the goal of only telling the story. Describing how a specific item or service made a difference is enough. Where to get it and how much it costs is not relevant to the story.

If you're following rules 1 and 1-1, the feeling of needing to sell will fade.

As product stories – and the stories of the product (how it came to be) – become more prevalent, story writers will become more in demand by large and small organizations alike. In-house marketing departments will want to add them to the staff, and small businesses will want independent writers to craft their stories for the most powerful impact.

The value independent writers add to story writing is the outsider perspective. Organizations, like individuals, lose sight of their own abilities and can become blind to what would make a good story. The successful story writer can see the power of an event that the organization may see as merely being day-to-day. Someone once asked me how they could learn that skill and my first thought was, "huh?" Outsider perspective is not a skill; it is a fact. However, being observant and empathetic are traits that you can build up to improve your ability to spot a great story.

Technical Writers

The User Guide for the first VCR my mom owned had a very simple cartoon on the back: Superman sitting on the floor, legs crossed, looking cross (or confused), with a book in his lap. The caption: "If all else fails, read the instructions."

If instructions were not so difficult to understand, more people would read them!

To be fair, technical writers do more than write instructions. They write about the how, where, and why of a product. Everything from "what does this button do?" to the logic or reasoning of the process that happens when you push that button.

A good technical writer understands the product and how the user will interact with it (which is frequently different than how developers interact with a product). With that understanding, the writer can explain how to best use the product to achieve the desired results.

What really makes a technical writer good is the ability to explain the same thing, in multiple ways, without making the reader feel stupid. And that is a fine balance because you have to include every detail, and every detail can get boring.

I was successful as a technical writer for two reasons: first, I wrote the documentation I wished someone would have written for me; and second – I always kept that cartoon of Superman reading the instructions in the back of my mind. If people were reading my writing because they were annoyed, I didn't want to make the situation worse.

K.I.S.S. (Keep It Simple [for] Stupid) is a good rule of thumb for technical writers. Get to the point quickly and make the point clearly:

1. Because Superman is not regularly reading the manual, he wants to know the answer to his question RIGHT NOW. Simple steps to walk him through the process are vital.
2. Plain language reduces the odds of someone misinterpreting.
3. Pictures of what you are describing go a long way in technical writing; that way people can compare what they should see with what they are actually seeing.
    - ➢ Anyone who has assembled furniture from Target or IKEA knows that completely replacing words with pictures is not a good solution.
4. Document translators generally charge by the word; therefore, the fewer the words (without losing clarity) the better.

Technical writing is a solid field to go into. Gadgets and software are always changing, and those changes mean that the documentation needs regular updating.

The popularity of staff technical writers depends on the economy and what country you're in. I have some very strong opinions about culture and documentation. To avoid a rant, however, I'll sum it up like this: the best technical writers are from the culture they are writing for.

I did technical writing as a staff writer, so I cannot report on how it works for independents. However, working the many six-month (or so) contracts frequently available can provide a nice balance between regular pay checks and picking topics. Or, working on several smaller products at once can be a good way to be an independent technical writer.

Electronic Communications

Anyone born after 1980 is probably thinking something along the lines of, "There's another way to communicate?" I'm not that much older, and let me assure you that, YES, paper still has value.

That said, it is probably safe to assume that at least a simple majority of writing never sees hard copy.

Because so much of what we read – especially marketing – comes on a screen, here are some basics writers and clients ought to know:

> ### *Food for Thought*
>
> "It's been an awkward time for teachers, who have the task of pointing out to their inernet-savvy students that this is a transitional moment. The old order still rules, and has to be respected. Omitting an apostrophe may not cause a problem in a text message, but it can cause a huge problem in essays, job applications, and other kinds of formal writing. Not because it makes meaning unclear, but simply because it goes against what society considers to be acceptable English. Students have to be taught how to manage this situation, so that they know what's expected of them"
>
> — Professor David Crystal

1. Get to the point!
    a. Reading off a screen is hard on the eyes.
    b. People have short attention spans.
2. Pictures are good.
    a. People have short attention spans.

3. Links are better.
    a. It is likely that you are trying to drive traffic to a website, so make your content do that. This means more than just providing a link to the site; you want the reader to want to go there. Forcing the issue by cutting a sentence off in the middle is allowed. (It's called "teaser copy" in the marketing world – it teases the reader into clicking on the link to read "the rest of the story.")

Writing to Explain

Written explanations are difficult. You need to balance the knowledge of the expected audience with the lack of knowledge of everyone else who might read it. You need to be clear without speaking down to the reader.

Explanatory Writers

(NOTE TO READER: I made this type up! I came up with this type of writing to explain to people what I do. Google does have entries on explanatory writing, and there is overlap in the definitions; however, this is MY definition for MY made-up category of writing.)

In many ways, all writers are Explanatory Writers. If you're making (or want to make) money as a writer, you are conveying information through the written word. And, for the most part, the point of written communication is to explain something. Let me put a finer point on this.

Someone who translates an expertise into common language is an Explanatory Writer. We don't all need to know what the expert knows, but we need to understand some basics so that we know we've got the right expert. The problem with experts is that many of them lose the ability to communicate with non-experts. This is why I believe that many PhD holders should not be allowed near undergraduate students. When a person is so far ahead of the rest of us, it can be difficult to close the gap without an intermediary – the Explanatory Writer (or a graduate student, when in the educational world).

Many people would consider Marketing Writers to be Explanatory – and they wouldn't be totally wrong. Marketing is generally about explaining why one product, service, or provider is better than another. However, good marketing appeals to a person's buying instinct, and that is not the point of a good explanation. Now, a good explanation can justify a purchase based on emotion (the basis for all purchases), but good marketing explains and nudges the emotions.

An important rule for Explanatory Writers – and I thank Mike Plaster of *Plaster Consulting Group* in Snoqualmie, WA, for pointing this out explicitly – is to keep the writing conversational. "You can create content with all of the necessary information, all of the supporting details, etc., but if it's not engaging, you won't hold your audience," says Mike. And, as any writer will tell you, the LAST thing you can afford to do is lose your audience.

I don't know of any company hiring Explanatory Writers (no matter how much they may need a dozen). So, this is an independent gig.

All in all, I find these quotations brilliantly apply to the mindset of an Explanatory Writer:

"Any intelligent fool can make things bigger and more complex... It takes a touch of genius – and a lot of courage – to move in the opposite direction."
– E. F. Schumacher

"You do not really understand something unless you can explain it to your grandmother."
– Albert Einstein

Medical Writers

I wouldn't have been able to consider this section if it were not for Stan Mehr, Founder of *SM Health Communications*, in Newtown, PA. Thank you for the peek into quite a specialty!

Medical writing is not to be taken up lightly. A huge amount of knowledge is necessary before writing begins – knowledge that, as a writer, you cannot fake. You may not know everything you need before you start, but you can bet you will before you finish.

This field has a wide, sophisticated audience with distinctly different levels of understanding, or interest, in the topic at hand. It is entirely possible that one article targets health insurers, physicians, and policy makers; and it needs to engage them all. The ability to collate clinical reports, corroborate evidence of effectiveness or safety, and cite while translating complex medical studies is not for the faint of heart (or stomach).

Instant gratification is not something medical writers experience. While fact-checking is important in any field, the medical and legal scrutiny required for health-related publications – even those for internal use by a biopharmaceutical company or agency – is intense. The writer must reference and annotate any new information to correspond with the original source. Prior to publication, manuscripts undergo peer review and/or a grueling (and time-consuming) process called medical-legal review.

Personally, I think that is a good thing. There are always idiots out there who can manage to kill themselves with the information in an article, regardless of disclaimers. And those idiots have family members who will want to sue.

Kidding aside, the review medical writing undergoes protects all parties involved: the subject of the article (a pharmaceutical manufacturer, say), the person or organization that commissioned the article, and the author. Before publication, the review process aims to minimize legal liability, ensure opinions align with those of the publisher/sponsor of the article, and validate the credibility of clinical evidence and other references cited. So, while multilayered and frequently diluting, the review of medical writing is really in everyone's best interest.

Good journalism is the starting point for medical writing. However, good journalism can also be a challenge for medical writers. For example, health care publications that accept advertising (and most do) must walk a fine line between balanced arguments and advocacy for an advertiser or potential advertiser. These trade journals offer some of the best opportunities in the business, but may require the most care to preserve objectivity. This can make an unbiased article that presents all the viewpoints difficult. Or, it could be just the challenge you're looking for.

Stan tells me that it is possible to be an independent writer in the medical writing field. However, I've got to say that the additional resources available to the staff medical writer sound much more appealing to me. Either way, passion for the subject matter is a must to be successful.

Science Writers

Shayna Keyles is the PR Coordinator and Contributing Writer at *GotScience Magazine*. As the name implies, *GotScience* is about translating "complex research findings into accessible insights on science, nature, and technology" for the general public – and they do it for free.

One of the main obstacles for science writers is scientists. Well, the relationship between scientists and writers. Unfortunately, generally the writer is the source of the problem because we forget how science works. While we can thank science for the age of instant gratification, the scientific process is as far from instant gratification as possible – it is about trial and error, discovery, and taking innumerable small steps before the big breakthrough. When journalists skip the steps and oversimplify the breakthrough, it is easy to see how the scientist might not want to deal with journalists in the future.

The science writer who keeps being a science writer develops a trusting relationship with scientists by being informed on the subject beforehand, showing respect for the work and the individual, and doublechecking everything before publication. Overall, the successful science writer treats the content with integrity.

> *Food for Thought*
>
> "When writing about science, don't simplify the science; simplify the writing."
>
> — Julie Anne Miller, former editor of Science News

The trick becomes balancing content integrity with keeping readers engaged. Whereas a traditional science article begins at the beginning – the hypothesis – and works its way through testing and finally results, that structure does not generally work for the nonscientific community. To grab and hold the interest of the reader, science writers tend to start with the conclusion – with the appropriate background – and work their way to the beginning: what were the results, then how the researcher attained them. No matter the order, the science writer always has the audience in mind when presenting information – avoiding complex terminology and clearly explaining it when avoiding it is impossible.

Integrity and information are what make science writers successful. The first is a personal trait that is best when it comes naturally. Unfettered access to the second is a bit harder. You want to make sure that the people who have the answers you need are not only available, but that they will thoroughly answer your question the first time and not become too annoyed when you keep coming back for clarification. Face to face or telephone conversations generally make this easier.

Writing for Individuals

These are the "get cozy with your client" writers as they require a much deeper knowledge of the client to produce the desired results.

Resume Writers

Number 2 of Lorrie's 3 Commandments of Writing is, "People should not have to write about themselves." Resumes are a big reason for this.

According to my favorite online source, dictionary.com, a resume is "a brief written account of personal, educational, and professional qualifications and experience, as that prepared by an applicant for a job."[1] A sterile definition that doesn't even come close to all the nuance necessary for a modern resume.

A resume is a personal marketing piece. The accompanying cover letter focuses on specific experiences applicable to the reader and adds the POW of truly great advertising. To be able to do all of that for yourself is generally unrealistic because we (as people) do not see ourselves or our accomplishments clearly.

A professional resume writer needs to be part marketer, part advertiser, and part psychic to see into the minds of hiring managers – especially since they also tend to write cover letters and online profiles.

As Katherine Akbar, President of *Your Edge for Success YES LLC* in Alexandria, VA, put it, you need to "create a little drama in the cover letter lead and then ride the client in on a white horse to save the day." This is not a skill you find in most nonfiction writers.

Because one size does NOT fit all when it comes to applying for jobs, resume writers need to craft multiple versions of the "same" document to highlight different skills and experiences for specific job titles, industries, and keywords. Again, not an easy task, especially, as Katherine says, "if the client is changing fields, and you need to highlight the relevant skills and tweak the wording to make it seem even more relevant while eliminating some of the irrelevant material. Sometimes you

---

[1] http://www.dictionary.com/browse/resume

have to take an unconventional background and portray it as a unique advantage—[and] cleverly disqualify the competition that does not have that background."

To be a truly great resume writer, you need to work closely with people and be able to pull out what makes them unique – while they're telling you there is nothing unique about them. As I said, most people do not see what they do as being particularly special. You can learn ways of getting information out of someone, but if you're not already a people-person, I would not recommend this field – as either a staff or independent writer.

Speech Writers

Commandment #3 of writing: Just because you speak brilliantly doesn't mean you write brilliantly. I say that because writing an idea takes a different part of the brain than speaking it. So, just because someone is great at delivering a speech does not necessarily mean they can write one.

"I've heard speechwriting referred to as a 'dark art'. People think that speechwriting is an innate skill that you're born with. But it isn't. It's something any writer can learn with practice, perseverance, and a great teacher," says Felicity H. Barber of *Thoughtful Speech* in San Francisco, CA.

Logically, I'm sure that's true. Emotionally, I'm still in the "dark art" camp.

That said, I think Felicity would be a good teacher; she certainly was able to explain the basics to me in a way that satisfied the Clear Communication criteria – a task not always easy for people when discussing their own expertise.

Writing for other people is a collaborative act. This is especially so for successful speechwriting. You need to be able to accurately represent your speaker, as well as the person's story and message, in your final product. That means that you need to get to know your client and draw out all the gory details.

(NOTE TO READER: If you are going to have a fit about my split infinitive, I'll have you know that splitting an infinitive is physically impossible in Latin and the "rule" was added to the English people by a bunch of snobs who thought everything Latin was cool.)

> *Food for Thought*
>
> "Forcing modern speakers of English to not – whoops, not to split an infinitive because it isn't done in Latin makes about as much sense as forcing modern residents of England to wear laurels and togas."
> — Steven Pinker

Now that you have a pile of stories, messages, and impressions of your speaker, you get to make a coherent speech that engages the audience. Knowing the audience is important so that you can phrase the speech appropriately to the group. You can tell the same story to a room full of CEOs that you tell a room full of 3rd graders; you just use different words to draw the picture for them. No matter the words, a beautifully drawn picture is required, because the more the audience connects with the speaker, the more engaged in the speech they will be. Action verbs and a wide variety of adjectives are important.

The truth is that while you could successfully tell the same story to CEOs that you tell 3rd graders, you don't want to – their interests are a little too diverse. Better to pick the stories that will resonate the most with the specific audience.

Every speech has a single message – even the State of the Union given by the President every year. In that case, the message is "Things Are Great and Can Be Better" (you don't want the voters to think poorly of their government). The actual states of the economy, education, foreign entanglements, and so forth are the underling facts supporting the message. Luckily, State of the Union speeches are not the norm, allowing both the speaker and writer to focus on a more specific message.

Specificity in the single message is good and could be the hardest thing to get out of your speaker. Be firm with your client on this; it is harder to confuse the audience when you stick to one clear point.

Finally, the stronger the structure of the speech, the bigger the impact on the audience. We've all heard, "Tell them what you're going to tell them. Tell them. Then tell them what you told them." Personally, I first heard it when learning how to write thesis papers. It is also sound advice for putting a speech together. When the audience knows where they're going, get there, and then look back at the path, they are much more likely to remember the speech, and its message.

Yep, still sounds like a dark art to me.

Because there is a market for speechwriters, it's a good thing there are other people who write speeches. It's also good that speechwriting is not just for politics. Felicity wrote speeches for the CEO and executive team of Lloyd's of London before going independent. No matter who you write for, the primary difference between working on staff and working for yourself is the type of relationship you are able to build with the speaker. While staff writers get to develop a deeper relationship with their speakers, independent writers get to work with a wider variety of people and topics.

Travel Writers

Special thanks to Gil Zeimer, Owner of *Zeimer's Advertising Shoppe* in Tiburon, CA. I hadn't considered travel writing until I saw that Gil considered it a specialty – then I HAD to have it. I've since had a couple of occasions to meet Gil in person, which has been an extra and fun bonus.

Not often known for their entertainment value, travel books tend to be a collection of what, where, and how much, with a somewhat neutral description – just the facts. What keeps travel publishers in business is the fact that accommodations, dining, and shopping establishments open, close, and re-locate with some regularity, prompting updated versions of the book.

That is not the type of travel writing I'm talking about.

I'm talking about the travel writing that describes the experience in a way that so engages readers, they book a trip as soon as they finish reading.

> ***Food for Thought***
>
> "As a tourist, you become economically significant but existentially loathsome, an insect on a dead thing."
> — David Foster Wallace, Consider the Lobster and Other Essays

A travel writer's strength is in his or her ability to describe. Descriptions are not the same as instructions. Good descriptions evoke an emotional response. And if you want that response to be something other than, "What the <insert your favorite expletive here> is this person talking about?!" use language befitting the audience. For example, when referring to the quinquennial migration of some cute water creature, you would probably have more success with, "This species' migration pattern only brings it to this location every five years."

As many of my contributors also noted, Gil suggests adding a touch of humor. His approach is to highlight some of the more amusing moments of his own experiences – such as meeting, and falling in love with, a male humpback whale during his honeymoon. After all, travel is supposed to be fun (if not the actual travelling) and personal stories go a long way toward making a place more interesting to others.

Travel writing is a narrow field, so unless you can land a position with a well-established publication, you are most likely to do that type of writing as an independent. Gil feels lucky to have published a couple dozen articles in travel magazines, and he is quick to note that he's made very little money on those compared to the other types of writing he does. On the other hand, the "fringe benefits" of client-sponsored trips to exotic locales or tax-deductible excursions to scuba dive or ski around the world for research are well worth consideration.

To Edit, or Not to Edit – Is Not the Question

Let me make something excruciatingly clear: all writers need editors, and those editors CANNOT be an alternate personality in the same brain. That is the reason for Commandment #1: If you wrote it, someone else needs to read it before it goes out.

Why does writing need editing?

OK, the obvious does apply here. Typos, misspellings, and bad grammar are the easy answers for why anything written needs editing. However, most spell/grammar checks will alert a writer to the worst of those. And going back over that email message you just dashed out can catch a huge number of errors.

> *Food for Thought*
>
> "No passion in the world is equal to the passion to alter someone else's draft."
>
> — H.G. Wells

The obvious reasons for editing are more about reviewing and less about actual editing. There are two screaming big reasons for editing: 1) writers stop seeing what they wrote and start seeing what they intended; 2) just because something is obvious to the writer does not mean it is obvious to readers.

What You Say v What You Mean

People generally know their message when they're writing. The problem is that getting the words right takes time – sometimes the first way you put something down doesn't quite convey what you really want. It could be choosing the right tone, words, or format. After a while, the brain decides it has had enough and declares that whatever it is you have on the page is right.

That switch in the brain is a mystery to me. Is it based on time, your expertise on the topic, how many martinis you had the night before, or what? Yes. I suspect all of those things – including "or what" – play a part. I also suspect that someone has put some study into the matter, and I just haven't seen the results yet.

Something else I've discovered is that the more important the item I'm writing about, the harder it becomes to switch my brain back. That's one reason I only submit drafts – my clients are responsible for the final product. And when it comes to something I've written for myself, I get someone else to read it.

But That's So Obvious

Actually, probably not. A brick wall is obvious, but who writes about brick walls?

When you become an expert, the basics can seem obvious. But that's because You. Are. The. Expert. The rest of us are not experts and may not even know the basics – that's probably why you're writing. Again, think about all those PhDs confusing undergraduate students around the country.

Similarly, when working on your own story, things can seem obvious because they've always been that way for you. Note the "for you" part. We all live different lives and have different perspectives; what's normal for me may seem dramatic to someone else. (Actually, normal for me is abnormal to most.)

Having someone else go over your work can catch those references that make sense only to you.

Why an Editor?

Although having someone review your written work is a good idea, it is not the same as having your work edited. The right type of editor will ask questions that help you clarify, not just what you wrote, but what you actually meant. An editor will also help you explain those things that seem so obvious you don't know how to explain them.

What Do You Mean, "Type of Editor"?

Frequently, writers are also editors. Since writing and editing fall in the same Clear Communication bucket for me, I went looking for some other opinions about why some people do one, others the other, and still others both. (Think about it; it does make sense.) Almost instantly, I found exactly what I was looking for on dailywritingtips.com. Author Mark Nichol made this distinction between writers and editors:

> *The writer is generally emotionally invested in the work. It is his or her idea, or an expression of or a response to another's idea, and it often is marked with the writer's name. It belongs to the writer. The editor, on the other hand, is dispassionate — more or less interested in, perhaps even enthusiastic about, the topic, but not possessive. The manuscript is a puzzle to work out. The editor has professional pride and a desire to enhance the writer's efforts and make the piece the best that it can be, but this is done at an intellectual remove.*[2]

The emotional investment is a big reason why I try to have someone else edit my work. For a multitude of reasons, the writer and editor of one piece needs to be different people;

---

[2] https://www.dailywritingtips.com/whats-the-difference-between-writing-and-editing/

many of them boil down to emotion. It is preferable that those emotions do not get in the way of the writer/editor relationship, but don't count on it.

Just as there are different types of writers, there are different types of editors. Knowing what type of editor you are – or need – can prevent headaches down the road. I know this because it used to drive me nuts when people asked what type of editor I was.

Because my "formal" training in putting words together is fairly minimal, I didn't know that there were different types of editors, let alone what they were called. Editing was just the process of making written text better – I didn't categorize it. Thus my annoyance at "What type of editing do you do?" The transition from not knowing what I don't know to knowing what I don't know can be a kick in the pants.

Once I was aware that different types of editing existed, I then had to figure them out and decide where I fit in. That, actually, turned out to be easier done than said because, about the time I had the realization, I stumbled upon something that defined several types of editors. <Insert Snoopy happy dance here>

After more research, I now know that the exact description and name of editor-types can vary, but I find that most people understand what I'm talking about (more or less) when I use the terms Developmental, Copy, and Line.

Before defining them, I want to stress that all types of editing are about making written text better.

As Jeff Braucher, *The Santa Fe Word Doctor*, out of (you guessed it) Santa Fe, NM, put it, editing is about "making your client's writing clear, concise, correct, and consistent. That includes fixing redundancies, ambiguities, illogic, wordiness, and ineffective diction, rewriting a sentence when necessary, and occasionally moving a sentence or paragraph to a more logical location."

Mike Plaster, who also edits, adds that, "Editing is far more than proofreading. Yes, finding and fixing errors is part of it. But editing is more about examining content with a critical eye, asking questions and making the content better. This can mean restructuring and reorganizing. It can mean rewriting entire sections." He also appreciates that editing can be harder than writing from scratch – something many people fail to understand.

Developmental Editing

This is big-picture editing. Does the content (story) make sense? Are things consistent? Does it read well for the intended audience?

This can be truly bloody editing because this editor moves – or removes – entire paragraphs and questions everything. People also call this Substantive editing (and some people call Substantive editing Comprehensive editing).

The line between Developmental and Substantive editing is not subtle but rarely acknowledged. The Editors' Association of Canada[3] drew it most clearly for me. Developmental Editors are involved with a project before there is even a project to edit. They help authors develop the work. On the other hand, a Substantive Editor comes in once there is a body of work to edit for style, clarity, order, and all that other bloody stuff.

> **Food for Thought**
>
> "Editing might be a bloody trade, but knives aren't the exclusive property of butchers. Surgeons use them too."
>
> — Blake Morrison

---

[3] http://www.editors.ca/hire/definitions.html

I cite the Editors' Association of Canada because their site was the first place I saw the distinction made between Developmental and Substantive editing. As I lean more towards the Substantive – meaning I'm not the best person to help you figure out what to write and how to write it – I like to give the Canadians credit.

That said, most of the time, I see Developmental and Substantive used interchangeably. Editors who do these two types of editing work closely with writers to make sure that what they write is actually what they want to say.

I like that Geoff Hart, overall communications guru out of Canada, describes the purpose of both Developmental and Substantive editing as "to make the document functional for its readers, not just to make it correct and consistent."[4] This validates my distinction about editing for readability (functional) which may not be grammatically correct.

These editors are also most likely to come into conflict with the possessive nature of writers. A piece of advice: Sometimes you will lose the argument; get over it. As long as the piece is accurate and understandable, let the writer win when it comes to word choice; after all, it is his or her name on the final product, not yours.

Copy Editing

I haven't researched why "written matter intended to be reproduced in printed form" is defined as copy[5], so I can't explain it. Based on that definition of copy, I used to assume I was a Copy

---

[4] http://www.geoff-hart.com/articles/2000/substantive.htm
[5] http://www.dictionary.com/browse/copy?s=t

Editor. However, Copy Editing is not simply "the process of making written text better," it's a touch more detailed. Copy Editors get a little more precise with the process. Grammar, spelling, syntax, punctuation, and fact-checking are all in the realm of copy editing.

In the same article about Substantive editing, Geoff Hart explains that Copy editing "is rules-based and concerned with grammar, spelling, punctuation, and other mechanics of style and the internal consistency of facts and presentation. Both types of edit [Substantive and Copy] are essential; they just focus on different issues."

While Copy Editors may question something an author writes, their focus is on clarity and readability over planning and development. This is why writers don't generally hire them until the project is closer to done.

Line Editing

According to Andi Marquette[6], Line Editors "are the anal retentive microsurgeons of the editing world." These people read less for content and more for precision. Is everything – grammar, syntax, punctuation, spelling, word usage or over-usage, etc. – absolutely perfect? If it weren't the computer age, this person would literally make sure every "i" had a dot and every "t" a cross.

I've read different opinions as to when a Line Editor enters a project; I'm inclined to go for as late as possible. You certainly do not want to get this person involved before you have your

---

[6] https://andimarquette.com/2013/07/13/different-types-of-editors-in-publishing-cont/

facts, figures, or story in place. Why go through all that work when you're still rewriting and moving things around?

If you're looking for a proofreader, find yourself a Line Editor.

So, What Kind of Editing Do I Do?

I am a Substantive Editor. Do not give me something you are not willing to have returned covered in green ink. I'll point out inconsistencies, rearrange paragraphs, rewrite or insert text, and ask you all sorts of questions. I edit for readability because I know that grammatically correct and readable are not always the same.

However, I will assume you know what you are talking about and not do your fact checking – unless I'm curious or in serious doubt.

That said, I think every editor does a little bit of all types of editing. I'll fix grammar, and I am adamant about the Oxford comma[7]. On the other hand, I keep the Word grammar checker on for the finer points and am dependent on the spellchecker available with every software package that uses words. That said, I use words that some spellcheckers don't know, and I regularly ignore grammar check suggestions about sentence structure. And because grammar check does not always understand context, there are times when it's wrong. Again, readable and grammatically correct are not always the same; a good editor knows the difference.

---

[7] http://www.dictionary.com/browse/oxford-comma?s=t

So You Want to Write and/or Edit

You've either made it all the way through this book, or you've skipped ahead, and you believe that you have what it takes (a significant bit of crazy) to write nonfiction without actually writing a book. I don't know if I should congratulate you or offer my condolences.

Instead, let me offer some advice, both personal and from my contributors.

In General

No matter what type of writer you are, there are some basics all of us try to remember.

Appreciate Your Value

Confucius probably didn't say, "Choose a job you love, and you will never have to work a day in your life," because jobs at that time were distinctly limited. However, regardless of the source the thought is worthwhile.

My point is that no matter how much you love writing, it is still a job – and you need to get paid.

Know what you are worth, and what others in your field in your area are charging. For staff writers, that's reasonably simple – most job sites have that data. For independent writers, however, an industry chart is not as useful.

Knowing your worth is not easy. Most people either dramatically underestimate or dramatically overestimate what they ought to be paid. Few of us appreciate our actual value.

Compare yourself to others in your area. Are you filling a niche that no one else addresses? How long have you been at it? Then price yourself accordingly. If you're working from a list of national averages, take your cost of living into account. I live in one of the most expensive regions in the United States; I have no qualms about my rate being higher than the national average.

Don't Take Yourself Too Seriously

Trust me, your clients (or bosses) are serious enough for both of you. Their ego is more important, if for no other reason than that they are paying you.

(There are several ways to read, "Don't take yourself too seriously." In this case, the emphasis is on the YOURSELF.)

Impress People with Your Ability, Not Your Vocabulary

I take being a Word Nerd seriously. I love learning new words and understanding where

> *Food for Thought*
> "For I am a bear of very little brain and long words bother me."
> — Winnie the Pooh

they come from. That does not mean that I sprinkle them throughout my conversation or writing.

It is important to know the verbiage of your industry and audience. However, buzzwords and words with many syllables don't make you look smarter – in fact, frequently they detract from your credibility. Additionally, they don't always mean the same thing to everyone. Unless you know, absolutely, that your audience has the same definition of a word as you do – or you define the word in your writing – avoid buzzwords.

Learn from Criticism

Whether you are on staff or on your own, others are going to have something to say about your work. Some of it will be useful for your professional development; all of it will be useful to the development of your thick skin.

There will always be criticism – that's part of why I tell clients that I only submit drafts; nothing is final until they say so – after that, they're the one receiving the critique.

A good way to avoid some standard criticisms writers receive is to follow these excellent rules provided by George Slaughter of *Onion Creek Productions* in Katy, TX:

a. "Nobody gives a s#t about you. You are not the story."
   Keep your ego and personality out of the content.
b. "It's not what you say, it's what they hear." No matter how good you are, someone will misunderstand.
c. "Tell it like it is."
   People who don't like the truth will still criticize you, but life's not perfect.

If You Love to Write, Then Write

...even if you are not getting paid for it.

If you are a paid writer, writing might be the last thing you want to do in your off time. Do it anyway. The more we write – paid or not – the more we improve our skill as writers.

I specifically asked my contributors if they wrote fiction or did other creative writing; some said yes, others said no. The ones who said yes gave examples ranging from novels to holiday letters. I know, however, that those who said no do actually write other stuff – they just don't consider it noteworthy.

As writers, we write. We take care in how we put our words together. That is something we must do, so do it!

As an Independent

There is a lot about business that I do not know. (Thank you for sharing. Now. Shut. Up.) One thing I do know is that doubt is more than common; it's expected. You do not need to know everything; focus on your skill set and ask your community for help with the rest.

Here are some basics that have come in handy for me:

Define Your 3 Ps of Business

Here's how I was being an independent writer without writing ... (well, until I went and wrote this book!)

Have a Purpose (and Market)

I am out to make the world more understandable. What's your purpose?

I don't really think I can make the whole world more understandable, so I focus on passionate San Francisco Bay Area professionals who are fun, pleaseable, and want to document their expertise.

Have a Product

(OK – I normally tell people I provide a service, but I needed a "P" word.) What, at the most basic and fundamental level, do you sell?

1. Types of writing:
    a. Copy (marketing, advertising)
    b. Content (websites, bios, blogs, articles)
    c. Ghost Writing (things with a byline/credited author that isn't you)
    d. Newsletters
2. Types of editing

Even if you do multiple types of writing or editing, be able to CONCISELY state what you do. "I can do anything for anyone" means you'll be doing nothing.

Better yet, knowing what you do makes you easier to hire and reduces the number of regrettable projects you take on.

Have a Process

Systems make life easier. My business is, basically, renting out my brain – not a simple or systematic thing. So, the more structure I have for creating my products the better. Newsletters are my best example of a systemized process. I have a process and all of my newsletter clients go through it.

Systematizing writing, however, is difficult. So systematize your business. The more systems you have in place for billing, keeping in touch with clients, doing your marketing, scheduling, etc., the less time you will have to spend on them and the more time you can spend on doing what you went into business to do – write! You'll probably go through several (take advantage of 30-day trials), will be forced into some, and fall into others. Keep the ones that work and let go of the ones that don't – even if they did once. For example, I went through several billing programs before I found one I liked. I've also made two contact management system changes.

Finally, implement a process for your work day and work week. When you regularly do the same types of tasks at the same time of day, you train your brain, and you begin to do those tasks better during those times. For the tasks that do not need daily attention, schedule them for the same part of each week. Again, they will become easier with the consistency.

> *Food for Thought*
>
> "If at first, you don't succeed, take the tax loss."
> — Kirk Kirkpatrick, entrepreneur

Version Control

I cannot emphasize enough how important it is to have a system – any system – for file version control. You send something to clients, and they send it back with comments/edits. You then need to work those things in and send the update to the clients. That is three versions of one document. Trust me: you want to keep and be able to reference all of them. Computers ask you if you want to overwrite a file for a reason. You are a person whose business depends on the input of your clients, which is why YOU DON'T WANT TO OVERWRITE A FILE.

Appreciate Your Value – II

Yes, yes, I've said this before. However, as an independent your sense of value has an impact on everything you do. If you do not feel you are worth the price you charge, several things can happen, the biggest being that people won't hire you.

Whether you charge by the hour or word, or you bid every project at a flat rate, people can see your confidence in your own skill and will judge your price with that in mind.

There will be a point when you just don't know how to price a project. It is common for projects to become bigger than initially thought – you find something interesting in your research, the client keeps adding things, or you just fall down a rabbit hole. Rather than looking uncomfortable and/or indecisive (I've done both), "bite the bullet and throw a price out there," says Molly Walker, Principal at *Walker Communications* in Oakland, CA.

Admittedly, I don't always have the courage to "just" throw out a price. I do, however, have the courage to say, "I don't know." This is when having an hourly rate comes in handy. With confidence, you can say, "Normally, I charge XX per hour. I'm not sure how much time this project will take. My experience tells me that it will be at least YY hours." This provides both you and the prospect with a starting point.

As your confidence grows, and you become established in your business, you'll be able to pull away from hourly rates and be able to quote project prices. The underlining base for a project price is how much you want to make for the time you spend; however, your time is the least of it. You are renting out your brain. You are providing a valuable service, charge for it – and then earn it.

And when someone questions why you charge so much for what looks like so little (and someone will), remember what Gil Zeimer said to the client about why an hour's work cost $125: "It took me over 30 years to be able to write something that quickly and that good, so she got 30 years of experience in one project." However much experience you have, it is more than your clients have; otherwise, you would be hiring them.

(p.s. Not only are they paying for your experience, they are paying you to deal with them. Some clients are easy; others are not. And then there are some clients you will never work with again, no matter what they pay. You are allowed to include an Annoying Client Tax to your prices – just don't tell that to your clients.)

Feel Free to Mix and Match

Most of the writers who contributed to this book do more than just one type of writing. In fact, independent writers frequently need to broaden their range to keep the jobs rolling in.

That said, I believe in knowing what you're good at and focusing on it. As you expand, keep to the things that are similar to your sweet spot. For example, I started as a technical writer. When I went independent, I realized that engineers were not the only experts whose language I could "translate" into normal English. That's when I declared myself an Explanatory Writer and that's where I focus most of my time. However, I do stray into some marketing work, and I've been known to help with a resume or two (explaining someone else's value). Speeches and grants, on the other hand, are distinctly not my department.

Protect Yourself

As an independent, you're likely to have to fill out a W9 form for many of your clients. That means giving your social security number to all of those people. Unless you have an Employment Identification Number (EIN). This is a unique number the IRS assigns you and ties your business name to your social security number. (The IRS already has your social security number, you can't get around that.)

> **Food for Thought**
>
> "In 1790, the nation which had fought a revolution against taxation without representation discovered that some of its citizens weren't much happier about taxation with representation."
> — Lyndon B. Johnson

It is incredibly easy to apply for an EIN. Just go to https://irs-ein-tax.com, select your business type (see the next section, "Get a Lawyer"), and follow the directions. I think it took maybe 10 minutes for mine to show up in my email.

Nobody wants to think that their clients are going to end up being bad people; however, bad things happen – even to good people. Giving yourself this layer of protection is easy, takes almost no time, and is free. Why wouldn't you do it?

Get a Lawyer

Are you a Sole Proprietor, LLC, or corporation? Do you even know what those things are? I've had multiple business lawyers explain them to me, and I'm only mildly comfortable with the definitions.

Going into business for yourself, even as a solo entrepreneur, requires some legal paperwork. Frequently, do-it-yourself legal paperwork is not worth the toner used to print it. Invest in a business lawyer to get you set up properly.

Because I'm cautious around anything legal, I asked my business attorney, Michael Schachter of *Pearson and Schachter*, what he suggests to those just starting out. Here are his top four:

Make sure no one else is using your name.

That is, your business name. A Google search is a good place to start. Buy your domain, even if you do not have a website right away. If your domain name is not available, you could be stepping on someone else's toes. You can also check the United States Patent and Trademark Office database (uspto.gov) to see if anyone else has already staked a claim to your name or logo. (Be careful, that site can be a bit of a rabbit hole if you're not careful.) Check your state's Secretary of State website to make sure the name is at least available in your state. There are search companies who can do all of this for you – for a fee.

Also, think about trademarking your name. Federal trademarks are preferable because of the strength of the protection they provide. However, if you plan on doing business in only one state, registering your name with that state's Secretary of State is probably sufficient and definitely cheaper.

Not a legal protection, but a supportive argument if your business name comes under dispute, is the fact that you are doing business. The argument is even stronger when you own and use the website domain. (It's also good to own your personal name domain, but that's more about controlling your image.)

What is your business type?

If it's just you and your bunny slippers, a Sole Proprietorship may be good enough. You will still want to file a fictitious name statement in your county. The problem with a Sole Proprietorship is that ALL of your assets are at risk if someone decides to sue you.

To separate your personal assets from your business assets, you can form an entity – either an LLC (Limited Liability Corporation) or Corporation. In California, the annual Franchise Tax Board cost alone is $800. Your state may be different in terms of the amount and frequency, but there will be a cost. And there will be paperwork to do annually.

Before talking to a lawyer to help you set up your business, talk to your CPA to determine what type of business entity would be best for you.

Protect your intellectual property.

This can get a tad fuzzy, seeing as how you are using your intellect to write for other people. Easy things: trademark your name and logo; and copyright anything published in your name.

The not-so-easy thing to protect is everything else you write. This is where your client contract will come into play.

Have a client contract – and have your clients sign it.

Personally, I avoid topics that I think could get me sued. That, however, doesn't mean clients won't sue you anyway. Especially if they think you are going to solve all their ills, and all you do is write a few paragraphs. For your protection, make sure your contract includes:

- The scope of work
- The name and entity type of your company
- How much and when you get paid and an option to charge late fees
- Limited liability clause – they are ultimately responsible for the content
- Disclaimers – you are writing paragraphs, not saving the world
- Indemnity – if someone sues your client because of something you wrote, it is not your problem

Some additional items your clients may want include:

- Ownership of the rights (including intellectual property rights) to the final product
- Protection if the material is not original (don't plagiarize!)
- Confidentiality – this could cover anything from the topic to the fact that you do your client's writing

Having a relationship with a business attorney can make the growth of your business much easier. If you decide to rent an office space, you'll want the contract reviewed. If you inherit Great Aunt Minni's millions, you'll want to set up an entity to protect your inheritance from a sue-happy client (never underestimate the litigiousness of your fellow American). If you take on a partner, you'll need agreements for that.

All of these business decisions depend on your specific circumstances, with the results varying from person to person. A lawyer can help you determine what the risks and benefits associated with each decision will be for you.

The Client Is the Boss – Until You Fire 'Em

Any independent writer can fire a client (fact); and there is a unique pleasure in that act that is hard to find in any staff position (opinion).

If you are a writer, you keep writing until the client is satisfied. If you edit, you have to remember that your client's voice is different from your own. In both cases, sometimes you have to let something go that you feel is horrid because it is what the client wants.

That said, just because someone is paying you doesn't mean you can't terminate the relationship if things are not going well. Make sure you receive payment for the work you did do, and be prepared to take a loss.

If I'm not sure about a potential client, or if the prospect is not sure about me, I offer a trial. Set a budget, do what I can within the budget, and – after payment – we mutually decide either to continue working together or stop – without any bad feelings.

The best way to avoid firing clients is to interview them before you sign the contract. Make sure you:

- Are talking to the person who makes the decisions; an intermediary only complicates things
- Know enough about the project that you feel confident in your ability to do the job

- Tell them your pricing
- Explain your work process, so they know what to expect (I make them sign a copy)
- Remind them that they are part of the process
- Provide a time estimate – emphasizing that it is an estimate
- Like them enough to deal with their unique and annoying drama

When someone balks, and someone will eventually, know that you did your best and that some people are just idiots. Then fire the idiot. <Insert evil grin here>

If you find that all of your clients are idiots, you may want to reevaluate your business.

For me, at least, one of the best compliments a client can give me is hiring me again. That's how I know I'm doing things right.

Continue to Build Yourself

Many professions require continuing education to maintain the right to be in that profession (legal, health care, insurance, finance, etc.).

Although that is not currently the case for writers, continuing to learn personally and professionally is really the only way to grow.

At some point early in this book, I said that it's good to have coaches. I have a referral networking coach, a business coach, and a brain coach. I also know several other coaches who are willing to provide the occasional piece of advice. These people are good at what they know and know how to help you get good at it too.

Before I started writing this, I officially got a writing coach. She gives me deadlines, acts as that outside set of eyes, suggests content, and challenges me.

Before being my writing coach, Sue was (and still is) a great person to vent with. Do not underestimate the value of being able to vent with someone who is in a similar boat as you. Independent writers have a habit of isolating themselves – making meeting other independent writers difficult. Even if the only thing you have in common is being independent writers, having a good relationship with at least one other writer is a lifeline for your business and your sanity.

> **Food for Thought**
>
> "I believe that if life gives you lemons, you should make lemonade ... And try to find somebody whose life has given them vodka, and have a party."
> — Ron White

Don't (Always) Work at Home

I say this for several reasons. First, I'm a firm believer in home being where I am able to get away from work.

More importantly, home has too many distractions: TV, comfy couch, bed, kitchen, laundry, kids, pets, etc. No matter how much you love your work, your home has something in it that you'd rather pay attention to – especially when you are not immediately in the middle of the part of your business that you love.

Finally, we all need to get out of our caves. Even the most distraction-free home office is still home. If that's the only place you are, how are you going to grow?

Initially, having somewhere else to work seemed impossible to me. I certainly couldn't afford to rent an office. I had a decent home-office setup, so that's where I worked. The distractions, however, just about did me in – especially the self-aggrandizing neighbor who had very loud phone conversations on his deck, just across the path from my office windows.

The standard home-office alternatives, cafes and libraries, came in handy. There were drawbacks, though. Working in cafes can be fattening and gets expensive – plus they can be noisy, have lousy seating, and (until recently) regularly didn't have enough outlets. The local libraries are quieter and frequently have better seats and more plugs – but if you're as ferocious a reader as I am, a building full of books is the ultimate distraction.

Finally, I managed to join Victory Workspace, a coworking space here in the San Francisco Bay Area. I'm not there every day, but it gives me a great place to get work done, gets me out of the house, and has increased my business. By working around other people – many solo entrepreneurs like me – I managed to grow my business. Yes, I got some clients. But I also met people who could help me, as well as a few that I could help as well.

The best part of Victory Workspace is that it provides a community. They hold networking events and educational programs, and their staff is brilliant at introducing the members to each other. In fact, that's where I met my writing coach.

The Rest: Don't Ask; I'm Still Working on It.

OK, as an independent writer, I find that I spend plenty of time and thought on many things that relate to my business, but I have very little advice to offer. Just a few of those things are:

Mindset. What is going on between your ears is the biggest hurdle.

This is where a business coach comes in handy – someone who will tell you when you are being an idiot, or self-destructive, or just a bad business person. Don't worry; we are all idiots, self-destructive, and bad business people at some point or another. A good coach gets us through those times with minimal damage.

Marketing/Advertising.

You need to get new clients, and you need to meet people who can send you new clients. How you do this is up to you. Personally, I prefer working by referral, so I do a good deal of networking.

No matter what, networking is a fact of business ownership. It does help get you out of your cave. Find groups that can support you and your business in different ways.

I am a big fan of BNI® (Business Networking International) – an organization structured around passing referrals to other members.

I also suggest a professional organization to help you keep up with what's going on in your field, provide support, and introduce you to other independent writers. This was actually harder for me than I expected. Whenever I found a group that seemed to fit my needs, it would dissolve. Even after learning about IABC® (International Association of Business Communicators), I was not totally sold until I learned that the San Francisco chapter has a subgroup for independents. Yes, I write for businesses, but a group of staff writers cannot offer the type of support and comradery that I was looking to add to my networking.

Because marketing/advertising is necessary, most of us do as much as possible for as cheaply as possible when starting out. However, the sooner you can hand that off to a professional, the happier you are likely to be.

Finances.

Make friends with your CPA. OK, get a CPA, then become friends. The first thing a CPA is likely to tell you is to keep business money separate from personal money. When you're starting out, that may seem like an impossible line to draw – do it anyway.

Staff.

Do you want one? What will your staff do to support your work?

Partners.

Partnerships can be loose alliances with others with whom you swap services, or formally established relationships.

Growth.

And that's part of how I got into this book-writing mess in the first place.

When it comes to the rest of the business ownership thing, here's my best advice: Hire out the tasks that you can; and get good advice for what you can't afford to outsource. What's left is what you want to be doing – if it's not, that's a different issue.

The Continuation of the Path

Even though my path has straightened out, I try to keep myself open to side trips – if not full detours. There is a balance to keeping your eye on the prize and aimlessly wandering through life. The prize – currently, your career as a writer – is important; however, the potential to miss something even more vital is great if you do not look around and enjoy life. I'm far enough along in my life to feel confident about this path; you, however, may have a detour or two yet to take.

Living on the Corner of What I Love and What I'm Good At

It's a good thing I love what I do, and I'm doing something I'm good at, because the rest of this entrepreneur thing can cause me massive freak-outs. (In case you haven't noticed.)

Yet, as much as I complain about some aspects of being my own boss, I am a Much Happier Person than I was as an employee or the Chocolate Lady.

As I said earlier, the detours have done me good. All that odd knowledge makes connecting with clients easier. I also have more experiences to pull from to ease that translation from expert to nonexpert.

(And I still shake a mean chocolate martini.)

Contributors

I cannot thank enough everyone who helped me out on this project. As to the formal contributors, know that they all gave more than I actually included or cited.

Clyde McDade
Beach House Creative
Graham, WA
clydecopy@gmail.com
253 394 2750
clydemcdade.com

Dalya Massachi, M.A.
Writing to Make a Difference
San Leandro, CA
DM@WritingToMakeADifference.com
510 786 7415
WritingToMakeADifference.com

Felicity H. Barber
Thoughtful Speech
San Francisco, CA
felicity@thoughtfulspeech.com
415 283 8142
thoughtfulspeech.com

Gene Braunstein
ComedyFaceLift.com LLC
Norwalk, CT
Gene@comedyfacelift.com
203 202 7986
comedyfacelift.com

George Slaughter
Onion Creek Productions
Katy, TX
georgeslaughter@comcast.net
832 437 9833
georgeslaughter.com

Gil Zeimer
Zeimer's Advertising Shoppe
Tiburon, CA
gil@zeimer.com
415 246 6072
zeimer.com

Jeff Braucher
The Santa Fe Word Doctor
Santa Fe, NM
jeff@santafeworddoctor.com
505 603 7406
santafeworddoctor.com

Katherine Akbar
Your Edge for Success YES LLC
Alexandria, VA
katherine@yeswriting.com
202 740 3032
yeswriting.com

Ken Wachsberger
Azenphony Press
Ann Arbor, MI
ken@azenphonypress.com
734 635 0577
azenphonypress.com

Michael Schachter
Pearson and Schachter
Walnut Creek, CA
mschachter@pearsonschachterlaw.com
925 464 7086
pearsonschachterlaw.com

Mike Plaster
Plaster Consulting Group
Snoqualmie, WA
mike@plasterconsulting.com
425 785 2167
plasterconsulting.com

Molly Walker
Walker Communications
Oakland, CA
info@mwalkercommunications.com
510 428 9291
mwalkercommunications.com

Randy Wight
Funny Bone Productions
Walnut Creek, CA
Act2Improv@comcast.net
925 957 6839
FunnyBoneProductions.com

Shayna Keyles
GotScience Magazine
shayna@scienceconnected.org
gotscience.org
scienceconnected.org

Stanton Mehr
Revisions Communications & Editorial Services
Newtown, PA
stan.mehr@revisions-editorial.com
845 641 7011
revisions-editorial.com

Sue Stoney
The Message Crafter
Pleasant Hill, CA
leesuestoney@comcast.net
925 334 2632
themessagecrafter.com

Sue Toth
Sue Toth Writing and Editing Services
Lake Hopatcong, NJ
sue@suetoth.com
973 362 5382
suetoth.com

Susan Shalhoub
Plum Editorial LLC
Orlando, FL
susan@plumeditoral.com
508 221 3993
plumeditorial.com

Additional Readers

The additional feedback I received from these "random" people in my life proved invaluable.

Bob Britz
Career Coach
Walnut Creek, CA

Elaine Betts
Business Coach
Danville, CA

Leslie Eisenberg
Victory Workspace
Walnut Creek, CA

Paul Wildrick
Business Coach
Orinda, CA

www.ingramcontent.com/pod-product-compliance
Lightning Source LLC
Chambersburg PA
CBHW031929080426
42734CB00007B/620

9781949643336